Jubal Rising

Books by Michael Simms

Poetry
    Strange Meadowlark
    Nightjar
    American Ash
    Migration

Chapbooks
    Black Stone
    The Happiness of Animals
    The Fire-Eater
    Notes on Continuing Light

Novels
    Bicycles of the Gods
    The Talon Trilogy
        The Green Mage
        Windkeep
        The Blessed Isle

Textbooks with Jack Myers
    Dictionary of Poetic Terms
    Longman Dictionary and Handbook of Poetry

Jubal Rising

Poems

Michael Simms

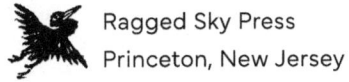
Ragged Sky Press
Princeton, New Jersey

Copyright ©2025 by Michael Simms
All rights reserved
Published by Ragged Sky Press
270 Griggs Drive, Princeton, NJ 08540
www.raggedsky.com
Library of Congress Control Number: 2024951283
ISBN: 978-1-933974-60-6
Cover and book design: Jean Foos
Photograph of author: Eva Simms
Cover art: Jane Bauman, detail from *Remnant/Detritus* series,
acrylic and fluorescent spray paint on paper, 22 x 30 in., 2018–2019
This book is typeset in Mundial, Essonnes and Inria Serif
Printed in the United States of America
First Edition

For Eva

Contents

The Skateboarder | 3

I.

Hookah Wink (Cup of Darkness) | 7
Halfway Prayer | 8
Jubal Rising | 9
The Lamp at the End of the World | 12
Dead Sea | 13
Forward Avenue Blues | 14
Nopales | 16
Renunciation | 17
William | 18
Political Poetry | 19
Ishmael | 20
Uvalde | 21
Unclenching the Heart | 22
Second to Last Testament | 24

II.

The World As Sound | 27
Persimmon | 28
You Taught Me | 29
Bookfair | 30
Happy At Your Expense | 31
Winter Morning | 32
Contagion | 33
"The Uncertainty of the Guest at the Feast of Our Writing" | 34
Dust and Shadow | 35
Forgetting | 36
My Brother's Hand | 37
The Street You Remember | 39
Tomorrow | 40
The Lighthouse | 41
I'll Wait For You | 42

III.

Magnolia | 45
Hearth Song for Danusha | 46
Edge of the Woods | 47
Hunger | 48

The Northern Forests Are Burning | 49
Closer | 50
After Fire and Flood Came the Singing | 51
The Deed | 53
Bloodroot | 55
Red River | 57
City of Ghosts | 58

IV.

Sweet Hatred | 61
Next | 63
October | 64
Black Stone | 65
More | 66
Red Mountain | 67
Maybe Swans | 68
Now That You Mention It | 69
Snow | 70
Now | 71
Understory | 72
Alien Lives | 73
The Bread of Forgetting | 74

V.

Chrysalis | 77
Dandelion | 79
Sun Star | 80
August Song | 81
Affinity | 82
Rain | 83
The Large | 84
Peony | 85
$D = \log N / \log s$ | 87
Turnip Love | 88
Turnip Greens | 89
Ecstasy | 90
Envy | 91

Before Leaving | 93

Notes | 95
Acknowledgments | 96
About the Author | 99

Jubal Rising

The Skateboarder

We feel a roar
Of vibration in the sidewalk
As we pass beneath the glass towers
Downtown, the fierce immediacy
Of the boy flipping the skateboard
Into, out of slides and grinds
Riding a steel handrail
While pushing the limits
Of resistance as he flies
What I remember
As a useless Christmas toy
And lands like a miracle on the sidewalk
Without colliding with startled pedestrians
Observing the usual rules
Of space and time
The boy inventing art from conversation
Between body and air
Bending the city to his delinquent will
An aesthetic of big pants small wheels
A lexicon of tricks and obstacles
Not sport but defiance
Not lifestyle but thrust and risk
A kick, an aversion to common sense
The danger practiced refined remembered
Until perfection is permanent, the body
Retaining music the way
Wings remember flight
And lament the return to earth
Where summer has begun
Balmy undefined felicitous
A suffering of desire
An impatience with the assortment of lies
He's left behind as he practices
A brave balance, his reflection fleeting
In the black glass of the window
He skates past the No Skating sign

An immaculate precision
In his rebellion no more personal
Than a summer storm I hide from
Beneath the canopy of my routine
I am what the skateboarder defies
His middle finger raised in salute as he rolls by
Does a quick ollie
Kickflip heelflip popping the nose of the board
In a backwards gingersnap between his legs
Sliding down the rail again
Arms held ready for balance
Falling a certainty
For the rest of us, not for him
What survives the plunge
Looks like anger
But it's art pushing his body
Into dark speed, precarious rapture

I.

Hookah Wink (Cup of Darkness)

I craved a cup of darkness
To smooth the mood
Untie the knot of my unrighteousness

So I stopped at the Church of the Golden Onion
Next to Gypsy Blood Tattoo and Rock Shop
Where glass pipes and hookahs wink
At the skanky junkie slumped at the register

Ah I thought one life at a time
Sat in a pew, opened the songbook and began to hum
The hymn of good intentions gone bad

The church was empty but full
Of the blue of Maria's robe
I lived halfway between pride and survival
A dumb fuck who couldn't admit he'd gotten life wrong

I was in a situationship with God—if you know
Then you know, you know? But all I knew
I was circling the dunny, ready for the deep dive

When this woman's voice came to me. It wasn't Maria
Our Lady of Sorrows, Undoer of Knots
But Maria Salvatore who hung at the corner
Husking and busking to make a buck

Need a meeting? she asked knowing I didn't know
But I did and we did and there we were
A little closer to getting through the night

Halfway Prayer

Jesus, I'm broken by anger
And need a fix of whatever
You have in your black bag
Of mysteries, holy magician
Of the forgotten, spectator
To the suffering that leads
Me to you. I need a trick
Of light that knocks me
To the asphalt, a summons
To the court of last appeal,
A bailiff who hauls my
Sorry ass in front of you,
Righteous judge of the quickening
Spirit, true witness to my
End and beginning.
Hey man of sorrows shining
Through the crack smoke
Don't corkscrew me no more
My soul hurts but I can't stop
Jerking off thinking of you,
Cringy lover, bunk mate
In this halfway house of the abyss
Show me how to rid myself
Of myself and begin again

Jubal Rising

Spider his momma calls him
Always spinning a tale
To make himself a hero

He hides a glizzy in his room
Little white street rat
He says *mooma stay*
Out of my zees you
Got no biz there fookin
With my shit so she

Slaps him so hard
His eyes bug and she says
Stop talking like a thug

She says *you come from good*
Folk who work hard she
Says *I'll die of worry you*
My baby and you going
Down the wrong road

And he runs out the door
Into the trailerhood
Of crackistan a bag
Of white skunk for sale
To the zombie at the corner

~

The man hurts the boy because
He enjoys it
Can get away with it
The boy bullies smaller boys
And those boys hurt
The smallest boys who swallow
A burr of self-hatred that grows tangled
And dangerous in the unforgiving sun

The drunken grandmother whips the boy
For being a mistake
He carries through the world
And children beside the road
Throw rocks at the passing cars
As if nothing matters at all at all

~

Jubal Momma says
You don't have to understand
Why the sun rises
Go about your chores
Noticing only
What's in front of you
Wipe the dish dry like so
Knead the bread like so
Let the living yeast live
And die in the dark
Not knowing they
Feeding you
Sit at the table
With those you love
Let them be
The light you live by

~

Grab a dime bag of certainty
Cause the streetlamp is an eye
Poked out / the better not
To see cash passed between
Self and self / ragged amen
For the chorus of young men
Hanging out the windows
Of passing beaters they borrowed
Cheering the hotties swaying
Down the sidewalk like
Well-fed cheetahs daring
The bangsters to try. Oh

They try awright. They bloody
Their noses trying. They say they
So high they never gonna die

~

Jubal pays attention
By not paying attention
Walking through the city haze
Far-fetched fantasia of broken
Brick and rebar pointing toward heaven
As if all he sees is the smoking city
Of regret and all-out suicidal romps
In the bad neighborhood of his head-scape
Where drinking drugging scheming
Collide with the law of fast returns
Karma ketchup he calls it because
Every action boomerangs back atcha
Wherever he goes he's there waiting
Ready to screw the pooch with lies
Deals and manipulations lined
Up from here to the jagged horizon
Of crack house nirvana. *Let's go*
He says. *Let's do it. Let's rise*
Like steam from a broken pipe
Let's be this frantic nightmare

The Lamp at the End of the World

How is it we love those
Who hurt us? Do they hate us
Or do they, as they say,
Hurt us because they love us?
Where did my father go
As he lay in the white room
Barely breathing? He'd become
Thin bones, nothing more
No longer a giant, no longer
A man who towered, swaggered
The balls of his fists hanging
From the chains of his arms.
How is it he became small
Like a weed, then smaller
Like a grain, then a speck
Of memory blown by light?

Dead Sea

Is it really wise to question a summary of a translation of a translation
Of a scroll found in a cave by a boy looking for his lost goat
When the alternative is the amber light that shines through a whisky bottle
In front of a mirror that holds my own face held up by my own hands?

The answer is *always maybe sort of* depending on who's sitting on the next barstool
And whether he's actually read the summary of Enoch's travels through heaven
Still alive to the possibility that a vision is a dream wearing suspenders.

Take Stanley here, part-time divinity student, full-time drunkard, fantasist,
Adulterer, who is sadly the wisest person I know, or at least the smartest
Person still talking to me when this tall guy walks in, only slightly older
Than me, but without the Dead Sea eyes like mine and Stanley's.

And the guy looks directly at me, or at least the part of me that's sitting here
On a barstool wasting my life, and he says *Are you Michael Simms?*
And I look around hoping for a twin separated at birth
But it's just me, Stanley and forty ex-friends, so I say *uh-huh*
And this guy says, *I have a poem for you* and I say *Okay Shoot*

And he recites a dozen lines about walking down the street right here
In River City and having an honest to god epiphany where the stars become
Brighter and the moon fuller and stained-glass lights the way to a door
Like Enoch entering heaven to find the inside is larger than the outside
Which is how I've always thought of Stanley and me and this whole scurvy world

And Mr. Epiphany, this angel (I think he must be an angel because all the other positions
Have been filled) having delivered his message, turns around and walks away.

I borrow a pen from the bartender and try to write down the poem
But it's gone. All I remember is the word *acquiescent* which Stanley says
Is not a word. *The word is acquiescence* he says but somehow the wrong word
Is the right word like the light coming from the mirror reflecting the faces
Reflecting the light from the moon reflecting the light from the sun
A million miles away. But somehow it's enough. Or almost enough.

Stanley and I sit for a while and he tells me he's been fired from his job
As assistant pastor. And then ten years later I get sober and have my own epiphany,
A half-assed one I still baby along like an old Chevy that keeps breaking down

Forward Avenue Blues

for Katherine Dunham

On Forward Avenue in those days
The BBQ King had a half barrel grill
Where he roasted chickens
Breasts thighs legs backs
Half chickens whole chickens
Take your pick. I was alone
Hadn't talked in days, not writing
Just watching television
In a stupor, games soaps
Cartoons comedies. *DYNOMITE!*
JJ Walker shouted to canned applause
In repeats of *Good Times*
About a family barely getting by.
Beside the BBQ King
A blind man in red shoes
Sat on the sidewalk teasing
A harmonica a *harp*
He called it gusting out
The blues improvising
A life. I bought a little dark meat
Leaned against a wall and listened
To the music panting uphill
Like a mean ole lonesome train
The BBQ King laid down
Chanterelles and portabellos
Roasting them quickly
On demand handing me
Salvation on a bun sauce
Dripping over the edge my
Fingers red and sticky
And the red shoes tapped
A rhythm and the harp
Called to a woman in rags
Whose smile almost explained
The long retreat that led me

Here where I felt more love
For this street chef and street
Musician I didn't know
Than to my own brother
A thousand miles away
Or to my sister teetering
On the edge of sanity.
Exhausted by the years of
Her story and mine
I wiped my fingers on
The brick wall I leaned against
Leaving red streaks like
Someone else's blood
Crossed and uncrossed
My arms not knowing
What to do with my hands
When a few more portabellos
Thrown on the grill
Made me remember
How invisible they are
As they grow from
The dark soil of desire
Bursting into air gathered
And roasted on demand
Slapped on a bun and slathered
With red sauce as the red shoes
Tapped a rhythm and the harp
Beckoned two plain-faced angels
Walking by hand in hand
Another couple lost to love

Nopales

We were driving across the dry plains
West of Austin. Miles and miles
Of miles and miles of cactus
What are those? My son asked
Prickly pear I answered
*If you ever find yourself lost
In the dry country
Break apart the leaves
And suck the moisture* I said
Pretending to know lots of stuff
They're edible? He asked *Yeah
The leaves are called* nopales
Have you ever eaten one? He asked
Hoping to catch me out
Oh yeah lots I said *in omelets*
How come I've never heard of them?
He asked. *Because anglos
Don't eat them* I said as if
We're not anglo mostly

This happened a year or so before
The compulsion, the erosion
Of soul began for both of us.
We were driving across Texas to visit
My folks in Llano. He'd spend
The summer with his cousin
Jumping off the rusty iron bridge
Into the river, taking girls to the movies
And driving a four-wheeler over the pink granite
Of the dry riverbed behind my parents' house.
It was Nicholas's last summer as a boy
My last summer of pretending
To know anything at all

Renunciation

The priest found a bullet
In the offering plate among the envelopes
And dollar bills. It didn't seem like a threat
But a renunciation
Of a life left behind, the way
A shepherd under the stars might have given
A ram's horn to the shaman
To call the elements to enter the space
They shared with the wind and the voice
Of the wind and the blood falling on the sand

William

Much later the quiet man
In a lavish room far from home
Spoke of goats on his beloved land
Interesting animals I said
Fascinating animals he agreed
But they don't belong in Hawaii
They destroy the native flora
And he spoke of the deep cries
Of whales   the cow in the rain
Who died down the road
From his house and the brothers
Tried to burn her then covered her
With dirt to be reborn they said
As grass   the eminent poet
Sat beside the window looking out
At the Hilton parking lot and beyond
To the blue towers he didn't recognize
And answering no question of mine
I'd ask for many years

Political Poetry

I think of the ruptured night watchman
At Wheeling Steel and the light inside the bodies
Of men at the glass factory where Wright's father worked
And Terman's father like Lear sweeping an arm
At the kingdom of his used car lot and saying
Someday this will all be yours. McDougall
Spinning small-town grief and gossip
Into American opera. Hamby
Juggling images while riding a unicycle on a tightwire
Of similes through the attic of a dictionary.
Somehow our private moments become
Public art, thrusting our viscera
At passing strangers, the music of words
Making them care

Ishmael

I'm not prepared to measure grief
Like grains of darkness

Who suffers more?
The man who sits in the rubble of his home
Weeping for his wife
Or the grandmother who walks by
Holding a broken doll?

The night sky is filled with menace
Tanks roll by at dawn
Who can measure sorrow?
Where is the boundary of mercy?
Which child is not ours?

Uvalde

The news is the same old
Murder of children
At their desks loving stories
About ponies and castles
Where so much happens
Between syllables we
Understand the unfolding
The swelling and collapsing
Of a small promise more
Tentative than we knew

But we're somewhere far
From the terror where a calm sets in
Like a breath held hostage
As in a garden of roses and sparrows
Where a cricket ratchets a rough lamentation
And a green tree frog remembers
An ancient elegy for the fallen world

Unclenching the Heart

Aldo was a chubby kid
Who played in the park down the street
Now he's a cop   a tattooed goliath
Curling 100-pound dumbbells
Face twisted with rage

Sometimes I wonder
What the hell happened to us

From a God's eye view
Baghdad must look like the ant bed
Carl and I poured gasoline on
Lit and ran. As long as we stuck
To our story, we'd never be blamed

When Carl came back
A dozen missions flown
We talked of girls
We'd kissed, plans we'd had
Half-sloshed I asked *how many?*
Carl looked in his beer and said
I did as I was told

How many children? I asked
None he whispered
But terrorists hide among families
So it's their fault

Walking downtown
I see a Gucci couple step over
Ragged children on the sidewalk
I give a fiver to their mother
Because some days life feels
Like one cruel act after another
And some nights I wake in the dark

But this morning Eva shows me a picture
Of her client K.'s college graduation
In prison where he's serving life
He's hugging his mom
Who forgives him every day
As he forgives her

And then I walk into Bud's Diner
Where Mandy in her pressed blue uniform, veteran
Of a million cups of coffee, nods and smiles at me
A regular iced tea and fries kind of guy

On TV I see Wayne Hsiung has saved
Two more sick piglets from a factory farm
And he'll do it again he says
The jury, bless their souls, finds him innocent
And Sweet Baby Jesus he *does* do it again

Second to Last Testament

Since I never cared about anything
But love and beauty
You can do whatever you want

With this brittle husk when I'm done with it
Let the body find its own bright scattering
Toss my ashes into the wind

For all I care, let them drift
Into the Mon Valley
To mix with the unpretentious love

Of the parishioners
At St. John the Baptist Ukrainian Catholic Church
Straight down the mountain from us

Where old women stuff pierogies
To repair the golden onion on the roof
And raise money for the orphanage

In their hometown of Vorzel outside Kiev
Bombed last month. Every Wednesday
They fill over three thousand pierogies

Bag them by the dozen, grab their mops and pails
And scrub the granite floor beside the sacristy
Until the priest is walking on light

II.

The World As Sound

I didn't speak until I was five
Because everything was sound
My mother's high heel was a slide
Her foot sang into. The rectangle
Of the coffee table was a clinking
Glass and a book that played
The violin. I couldn't speak
Because I was the scream turned
Inside out, a tree branch moving
Through the blue song of yesterday
The first time I heard a tango
I knew it was a purple rising
Through the folds of want

Persimmon

Nothing changed the first year
Although I felt the white net
Of mycelia spreading
Around roots and leaves
Learning to move through sunlight
And shadow the way I was learning
To move easily through the seasons
Because I couldn't speak. Each October
The leaves fell joining
The layer of humus. The wet leaves
Froze in the fall, decayed in the spring
Fed the new leaves in March
And all summer crickets sang
And also robins and in high pines
A crow called. In the third year
I saw a spoonbill fly overhead
Forming words out of air but no one listened
The sapling spread until it filled a corner of the yard
And we had to move the tomato patch
To the sunlight and later the garlic and parsley
I was supposed to be baptized
But refused believing only
The light and dark of the garden
Each year *Diospyros*
Filled out, growing lush and tall
In the sixth year flowers appeared
Then green fruit which yellowed
We spat the astringent flesh
And placed the basket of fruit in the cellar
To ripen. After a week, the persimmons
Hard crisp and sour as crabapples
Darkened, sweet as peaches
Dusky as plums and we ate them
Greedily all but one
I left on the windowsill, an experiment
In sunlight. The last persimmon
Was soft, a small black sac
I bit open and my mute tongue
Welcomed dark honey

You Taught Me

To listen without trying
To see without trying
To be here without effort
Letting words flow through
You with a sense of humor
Fascination being the rule
The guiding star in a dark
Field of star-flies which grow
From grubs you wouldn't
Admire even on a good day
Which came often in those
Days opening a textbook
On set-theory to explain
Grammar as if it could but

It could and the time you pointed
At the bubbles rising in the pitcher
Of beer to explain consciousness
Which was blurred by that time
Of evening you never said you
Wanted to kiss me until many
Years later when you were dying
And I was old and you were
Older what a pair we were
Bumbling through the department
Of tears when your old professor
Was dying and now mine

For John Lewis

Bookfair

There's a woman up there
Named for the first light
She's my friend for thousands
Of days although I've seen her
Only once   beside me
In a ballroom of poets you
Could guess each one's singular
Music by the movement of
Eyes over the stacks of books
Envy and ambition sometimes
Also sadness in the way the poets
Avoided touching shoulders
Sidewise through the crowd
Of crickets rubbing their legs
In crepuscular song

For Dawn Potter

Happy At Your Expense

In that moment after I cut you off
You winced, caught yourself
And forced a smile and I wondered
How often you forgive me
Without my noticing, how often
Am I thoughtless or selfish
Directing the conversation
Toward me, and you let me
Out of love, wanting me
To be happy at your expense.
How little my life would mean
Without you. Last night I dreamed
I lost you whether through death
Or abandonment wasn't clear
I wandered from room to room
The scent of you lingering
Like words almost said
Then forgotten. Outside
The deer had eaten the roses
Mist was tangled in the trees
A single crow noticed me
Cawed once and flew off
To join its tribe

Winter Morning

I wake to the light slanting
Through the window, the snow
Falling outside after a long night
Of resentment and loneliness

I rise, dress in jeans
My favorite plaid, my slippers,
Curious what will come

I adhere to exact rituals
A glass of water, a cup
Of coffee, farina with raspberries

I brush my teeth, inhale
My medicine, go to the keyboard
And surrender to the white page
Blizzard within, blizzard without

After a few failed attempts
I put on my boots, my parka
And step into the winter morning

Distant traffic, a train far away
The wind blows snow
Through blackberry canes
Thorns covered in ice

Contagion

What day is it?
I ask the old Black man
Walking carefully on the ice
In front of the hospital
January eighth he says
Stopping in front of me
A thin old white man
Shivering in my sleeves
I've been sick I say
He doesn't step back
Afraid of contagion
Instead he waits
I've lost four days I say
Confused by the bright light
Of the snow, the frozen
Cloud of his breath
Shouldn't everything be darker?
I wonder. *Are you feeling
better now?* he asks I nod
Congratulations he says
*Now go back inside
You forgot your coat*

"The Uncertainty of the Guest at the Feast of Our Writing"

—James Crews

I know we're supposed to look
And in looking, see, but sometimes
Life is cruel so we pretend
It's sweet even as our tongues burn
My mother was so kind
She clenched the lies to her chest
As the walls collapsed around her
She sat smiling and eating and eating more
Until her heart clogged and stopped
So I swore to always look
Pain squarely in the eye
Like a friend who says truths
I don't want to hear

Dust and Shadow

Pulvis et umbra sumus

When Klaus Spork the wisest man
I've ever known lay in hospice
He turned to his daughter my wife
And asked *Will you remember me?*
Always she answered. For forty years
He delivered groceries to the small stores
In the hills above Siegen. He never raised
His voice in anger. Faithful to simplicity
Klaus wanted only to be remembered
By those who loved him
Isn't this all? Only a few names
Survive. The rest becomes
Too quickly as Horace said
Dust and shadow. No illusion
Anyone will read my quiet rages
I want only those few
Who loved me to remember

Forgetting

In my mother's last years
She'd forget where she lived
Frightening for a homebody
Who loved to rock in her chair
Reading in front of the fire
Untethered from the familiar
Like a kite with a broken string

My father indulged her
Tender to the very end
When I was growing up
He never touched me except
With his fists so the last time
I saw him I took him in my arms
Gently like a bundle of twigs
I could easily break but didn't

My Brother's Hand

How small he was   my father
Lying in bed   arm over his face
Hiding from the red light
Of the vacancy sign   My brother
Looked down at our sleeping
Old man   my brother still
Speaking to me in those evenings
Of grieving   The river ran
Behind the motel   We could hear it
As we heard the highway
That brought us back here
Then we didn't hear
Anything but our father
Snuffling as he woke startled
And saw me perhaps

~

Kenneth and I shared a room
As we did long ago
Long talks under the dark ceiling
Of our father's anger as cars
Carried serrated light
Across walls into lives
We couldn't imagine   My brother
And I found ourselves together
By fate   both of us
On the spectrum neither
Had many friends so the cruelties
We practiced on each other
Were multiplied by loneliness

~

My brother hasn't spoken to me
Since we stayed in that cheap motel

In Llano Texas eight years ago
The silence between us a lonely road
I'm tired of driving

The evening sky used to be
A blue bowl with a red lip
I'm lying in bed on a summer afternoon
Remembering how we swam in the ocean
Waves from the deep lifting us toward shore
Our mother's voice calling us home

~

Where did they go
When my brother's hand
Poured them into the river
As he stood on pink and blue stone
Peculiar to this place of summer
As they were carried by rapids
Into the lake near the house
Where they lost themselves
To themselves many griefs ago
As we might lose ourselves
To the evening gathered in the trees?
Where were their bodies of ash
Carried, drifting through water, settling
Now in the alphabet of memory?

The Street You Remember

Often we love best what is lost
The hat with the crushed crown you left
At the wedding, the shirt you borrowed
With torn stitching and worn cuff
The black rock with the white stripe
You found on your last walk with the dog
You loved, the Chieftain tablet you left
In the rain, your large cursive rounded
Like clouds dissolving, the years lost
As well, especially now you are old
Your life is what is left behind
The street where you rode your bicycle
Throwing news in each yard

Tomorrow

Tomorrow I shall be
Or not   tomorrow is a face
In shadow   horizon
Of cloud   sunlight on a field
I'm walking through   A small house
Rises from memory   now
You're beside me   you've always
Been beside me   even before
Our life together   love began
Because it was always the door
Inviting us   the tomorrows
Are burning in the fireplace
The tomorrows never come
Yet always here the taste
Of tomorrow   a yeasty bread
The smell of tomorrow   the sweat
Of a horse   as we return
The sound of tomorrow   a sharp
Echo of a bell

The Lighthouse

I don't mind being old and not being able
To swim to the abandoned lighthouse anymore
Though I miss following the path along the cliff
With my dog, the two of us foraging
For lichens and enjoying the long view
Across the bay. The waves are quiet
This morning but you and I remember
When they crashed and yearned
As I do now sitting with you on the porch
The old dog sleeping at our feet
Our children in their homes
Far away, you take my hand and say
Nothing. The wide sky darkens, falls
Into the unbroken sea beyond the bay
Now evening joins us like a silent guest

I'll Wait For You

I'll row to the far shore
And when night descends I'll enter the city
And walk the streets of your absence
Find the small cafe we've always known
Where people are waiting as I am waiting
Reading a book you love

A thin man with a thin beard
Is playing a guitar and singing of a grove
Where he lived with a quiet heart

All night I'll wait for you
Sipping the darkness of his voice
And at dawn you'll arrive
Having thrown your luggage in the River Styx
And we'll drink from the silver cup of day

III.

Magnolia

Suppose you held what you love so tightly
You broke it
Suppose you let something slip away

Your eyes looking away at the very moment

The magnolia tree already dropping its petals
With each breeze

It was inevitable I suppose
The seasons rising and falling
The sky changing

Fourteen years since I've heard your voice
I didn't know you were saying goodbye

For Elizabeth

Hearth Song for Danusha

I can't tell you how much
This time together has meant to me
We held hands and crossed the frozen field together
We counted birds as they returned
We noticed flowers lifting their faces
To the sun. We felt joy
And praised each other even when we failed
As we had to, the secrets too heavy
To carry by ourselves. And you always
Shared your happiness, even when you spoke
Of sorrow, sitting in a chair, rocking a frail child
You knew was fading, even as you sang
To him, nothing was enough
And yet you sang and you sang again
And you listened and taught us to sing as well

Edge of the Woods

Let me imagine the edge of the woods
Where blackberries grow in soft light
Between bright grasses and dark
Pillars of trees and let me imagine
What might have been our childhood
If everything had been the way
Adults claimed and how
Strange years later they said the good
Years were back then always re-inventing
The peace they wanted to have won
And let me imagine light slanting
Down through leaves and a rustle
Of movement in the dark brush where
Luminous eyes of old fears
See us moving through the border
Of now between light and dark
Field and forest where we sleep
And travel a path to the house

Hunger

We don't want to think about
The child her eyes
Staring from the screen
Her small body carried away
We don't want to know
How close to the edge
We are   we want
To believe in the years
In front of us the path
We follow to the far hills
To rest beneath
A dying oak
Elm and ash
Gone   chestnut
With its wide arms of
Bounty gone   the hills
Scarred by the teeth
Of machines tearing the fabric
Of soil   imagine a child
Gathering wood for the fire
Bread cooked on a hot stone

The Northern Forests Are Burning

The northern forests are burning
And here 500 miles away
Smoke hangs over the valley
Tops of buildings like islands
On a white sea   the smell slides
Into our house like a virus
As we breathe toxins
So this is what it feels like
The end of the world
We know   White air
Brown water   So many days
Of getting and spending
So many arguments over trivia
Even poetry even love
Each morning listening writing
On the wire above the street
A line of birds silent in the smoke

Closer

We'd heard the world
Was ending so we lit
Small holes in the darkness
Lay down   held each other
All night hearing explosions
Closer til dawn
Silence like music
And then   birdsong

After Fire and Flood Came the Singing

Our iPhones told us
Of fires in the west, floods in the south
Great cities of the north and east
Erupting. Chaos everywhere
But here our neighbors stopped by
With gifts of strawberries in the spring
Tomatoes in the summer, squash in the autumn

And we in turn allowed our neighbors
To gather the fans of dark fruit
From the grandmother elderberry
In our backyard, and the stubborn blackberry
At the edge of our property, long believed
A weed, volunteered its abundance to all

That first year, our dog grew lean and happy
Hunting rabbits, squirrels and deer
The empty lots became wild fields surrendering
A bounty of dandelion, purslane and burdock
We threw away our iPhones
And rummaged books for remedies

The dark sky returned
And constellations long forgotten were known again
A blimp trailing the rags of a banner
Disappeared over the horizon
Then nothing but the godly sun looking down

And when the first generation was old
We learned to praise and only then
Ugliness left our lives
We gave thanks at the evening meal
Slept the sleep of the just
And woke to the sound of larks
While crows in the high trees called to us

A flute abandoned in the attic for years
Was lifted into song. In the evening beside the fire
We told stories of flying machines and moving pictures
Rusting hulls of automobiles
Were stripped of metal for tools
And tires were shredded to make shoes

And in the second generation
After we'd learned the language of larks
Trees began to speak
And we the people of the garden,
Began at last to listen

The Deed

Mart, Texas 1908

Someone who knew him called
His name and Chester came out
To the dog run between the two halves
Seeing no need for his shotgun leaning
Against the stones of the fireplace
And the man who used to live near
Didn't say his name and Chester didn't
Remember his name and the man
Told him to bring out his mother
And Chester did, holding the thin arm
Of the old Cherokee woman who
Rarely moved from her rocking chair
Beside the fire even in summer
The man held up a deed
You need to sign he said
What is it Chester asked *what*
Trouble are you bringing
She ain't done nothing he said
While his mother stood staring darkly
At the man her white hair braided
Are you working for the judge
Chester asked the man he'd known
From before but didn't know now
She gotta sign the man said again
This for her land near Spindletop
Chester asked *The land Sam Houston*
Deeded to the Cherokee forever
Chester asked   The man shrugged
Don't matter what's it for the man said
She don't sign Sheriff'll come
Chester remembered his shotgun
A .410 he used for squirrel leaning
Against the stones inside he looked
At Blue and Tick the hound dogs
Sleeping in the dog-run shade

They must've remembered the smell
Of the man from before cause they paid him
No mind *They gonna pay her*
For her land? Chester asked
But the man looked away at the field
Of cotton Chester and his 12 children
Farmed for somebody else then the man
Looked at the pretty roan grazing
In the far field Chester had given
To his oldest daughter Zelphia
They called Red for her hair
It's best your momma sign the man said
All the Indians are signing   And if she don't?
Chester asked casual-like as if making
Conversation not trouble
If she don't the man said
There'll be hell to pay the man looked
At Chester remembering when they
Was boys   *I'm real sorry about this*
The man said *but these men*
Are serious and they'll send hard cases
Out here you'll be lucky if they just
Send her to the reservation
As the men talked the old woman
Squinted at the man remembered
Feeding him corn pone and molasses
When he was a boy who ran
From his father   And Chester now
Remembering the bruised hungry boy
Watched his mother scratch her mark
And return to sit beside the fire
And wait for death to come

Bloodroot

Palestine, Texas 1932

For her all roads lead
To the shack beside the bayou
Her father glancing at his hand
On the wheel   the girl watching
The man's worry   the healer
Waiting for them somehow knowing
They were coming   her father
Unsurprised by the knowing
The girl in her green wisdom
Accepting the men's faith
In old ways   Without greeting
Her father held out his hand
Palm down the warts
Spreading on his brown wrist
The healer took the offending
Appendage muttered maybe
A prayer maybe a spell
Common in the bayou
Woods and farms   The healer
Rubbed the warts with his right
Thumb   cupping the man's hand
In his left   fixed his eyes
Speaking tenderly whether
To enchant or merely to pass
The time the girl couldn't hear
Then the healer let the hand drop
Refused the dollar the man
Held out   The man and girl
Drove back to town the girl
Pointing to the black smudge
On his wrist   Her father
Shrugged *it's the old way*
And years later the girl
Now a grandmother recognizes
The curvy lobes of *Sanguinaria*

And harvests the fat red
Escharotic roots near the bayou
Chops carefully grinds
By hand the blistering
Blood-like sap diluted with
Oak ash   a drop of olive oil
Like the remedy book says
As her granddaughter watches
Clutching a baby doll named
Serena against her chest

Red River

Bonham, Texas, 1963

She's returned, the woman
He killed twenty years before
He saw her in the face of a child
Who looked up at the tower
Of the church spire that seemed
To rise from the past in that city
Where he lived like a drunken monk
Writing every morning, drinking
Every afternoon until he passed out
He loved her and wanted nothing
But a tender moment of understanding
But she mocked him and he struck at her
Only once, his hand closed in anger
Shocking him and she fell back
Hitting her head on the edge of a table
Where they lived as a couple.
He hadn't meant it. He'd meant
To love her and somehow the passion
Turned ugly and he had become
In that single act a monster
And he left their home and became
No one, sleeping in alleys, beneath bridges
Below the traffic of ordinariness
Passing above and now thinking
Of her, he walked beside the river
Dark with insolence, unresolved
Weather breaking above him
And he came to a dead animal
A possum its belly open
To the flies and worms
Its tongue eating itself,
Returning flesh to earth and air
And he waded into the dark
And swam to meet her

City of Ghosts

When I return to the city of my childhood
Blue and gold buildings above the bayous
I'm not known even by my brothers
Who've carried their families
To different lives pretty boxes
In a crowded coffeehouse I tell a young man
How we seined a small pond
In this very spot I said pointing
At the floor my old shoes worn down
An old man ranting about trees
I told him I remembered frogs, turtles
And catfish we freed from the net
We kept the fish and killed the rest
All night fires burned in my window

IV.

Sweet Hatred

Out of spilled coffee grounds
And banana slime
Beside the compost bin
A gangly vine grew
Twisting
Out of shadow
Into slats of light
Between the boards
Of the deck above

I hated the way tough thorns
Of Rubus drew blood
Whenever I passed
The way a suckering root
Held clay and stone
In a thousand fingers
Never letting go / choking the softer roots
Of elderberry and cherry
Stealing water from roses and sweet shrub
And milkweed that fed the monarch

This bramble this briar patch
Of demon weed was killing my garden
So I investigated
Poisons / *triclopyr* kills
Dicots / leaving grasses alone
But would kill the roses
And azaleas and maybe
Me / but still I was crazed
With hatred for this weed

I scythed mowed axed
Hoed trimmed yanked
And eyed with vicious intent
This intruder eating my garden
But the satanic bramble would not die

Then in the spring of the fourth year of my war
The arching canes ventured small white blossoms
Whose yellow stamens attracted bees

And in midsummer green berries
Turned red then black
And a tanager perching on the compost bin
Feasted on the dark
Drupes / the berries tasted sweet
The hard seeds insistent on my tongue
I resisted pleasure / then succumbed

Next

There's a tic in my eyelid
Like a clock clicking off
The remaining light before
Darkness wraps its arms
Around me and carries me
To whatever's next. I imagine
A long line of naked souls
Moving toward the edge
Where we step into light
Beyond what we thought
We knew, beyond whatever
Small loves we embraced
Toward a great Adoration
That is and is not God

October

Do you hear the geese
High over the rooftops calling us
Back to ourselves? Do you believe
The leaves are aware of their changing color
As they move toward the final falling?
And autumn still promises winter
And winter follows winter into spring?
The first snow is a sadness always new
A promise the wind makes
As you pull your collar closer, resisting
What you most love

Black Stone

When it happened
I went deep inside myself
And found a round black stone
I could hold onto, polishing it
With my palms until it was smooth
As a mirror and I saw myself
In a quiet place next to a stream
Sycamore trees hung their branches
Over the water, shedding their bark
Letting the dry inedible fruit
Fall and be carried downstream
When I think how that older boy
Hurt me sixty years ago
Rage rises and falls and I need
To put my hand in the running water
Find the black stone and hold it
Until all is calm again

More

The mist that covers our mountain
Evaporates and becomes a feeling
That lasts all morning. You lift the spoon
From the sauce and feel the texture
Of the aroma. I love the way
You say silly things pretending
To be serious, the way you lift
The spoon almost touching your lips.
Steam rises from the pot.
Mist rises from the mountain.
All things rise merge divide
And merge again. We're old
And I want more of what we have.
Nothing different, just more.
Not forever. Just a few more years.
It's taken so long to arrive

Red Mountain

By now you're driving
The winding road between
Lake and mountain
The sky has opened
As a promise and you see
Your life in front of you
Curving through the white
Forest of birch and
The riprap of shattered
Stone above you not yet
Ready to fall

You've arrived at the cabin
From the days of your youth
Generations of animals staring
Out of darkness the door
Broken open by a bear
The mattress a nest of mice

You've returned to find
A place never there
Shimmering in memory
Like a poplar in late afternoon
You wonder how you survived
Alone among giants
How you lay in a boat
You found beside the lake
Floating like a cloud even now

Maybe Swans

I saw a flock of swans flying in formation she said
high in a vee moving southeast

Could you hear them? he asked

Maybe I could hear them she said
or maybe it was me imagining I could hear them
Trumpeter swans winter in Lancaster County
thousands of them floating on a protected lake

How far is Lancaster County from here she asked
Maybe two hundred miles?

Were they snow geese? he asked
they fly over and you can hear them

Maybe she said but I like to think they were swans
I wonder how they stay in formation for a thousand miles
Maybe they can feel each other move in the air currents
the roots of feathers have nerves you know
the way our skin can feel someone else close by

even if we're not touching? he asked

yes she said moving closer to him
especially when we're not touching
can you feel me now not touching you?

Now That You Mention It

To the inquisitive, I say
The soul is trans
Is whole   is turtle
Is nasty pure
Hazel smelling and
Forever yours
Or not

I was propositioned
By a man or
Was it a dandelion
Floating into
The next life
Or not
Or so
Or maybe I was dead

Maybe like wool
It felt like evidence
Felted by rain
Felt like soul
Aretha lives
In the dying

I lie down
In this accusation
Make it mine
Make it mention
Make it a long slow
Blue blonde
Kiss on the mouth
Why are we here
If not to be curious?

Snow

falls from the bright sky. A black dog digs through the drifts, finds a frozen egg and swallows it whole. Suddenly I'm awake, walking with the memory of you, noticing the porches ragged with ice, the Aeolian harp too heavy for the wind to move. The neighbor's red truck with its cargo of snow. A pile of cinder stones waiting for the trench to be dug. Three men warming their hands before an oil drum trash fire turn their faces toward us. As if by accident, we've arrived at the house of the half-chewed ball. The house the ball the memory white in the white air like a book with the cover torn off. Behind the upstairs window, an empty bed where a boy lay tossing with fever, his mother absent from the chair where she sat beside him for months, but now the black dog he loved is rolling in the snow with great joy

falls on the steeple of St. Mary's, clings to bare branches of the sycamore and coats the roofs of tall narrow houses of plumbers and waitresses. Flakes tick against the glass where the Southside High Homecoming Queen of 1958 now an old woman sits at her kitchen table sipping coffee remembering the smell of bacon frying in her mother's kitchen, her father sitting alone in his underwear having stripped off his blackened clothes and leaving them on the back porch, white skin of his legs, black dust on his face clearly belonging to two different men. And behind the house his clean white shirts frozen in the air

Now

You wonder what becomes
Of all that's seen and done
Not the big things   the birth
Of your daughter   forgiving
Your father   but the small
Goings-on   drying a favorite cup
Carefully   putting it just so
On the shelf next to the others
Lined up like the many days
Behind you   saucers stacked
News and music turning in the dance

What about waking next to the person
You love   how many thousands of joys
In that single moment repeated morning
After morning until today you wake
And she's gone   flying
Through the clouds on her way
Somewhere you didn't want to go?

Understory

I watched a show about mushrooms,
the quiet beauty of chanterelles
rising on the roots of trees
white giants like dwarves
in the forest puffballs parasols
the secret toys and umbrellas of
the understory   my story
invisible fecund
the dark spectrum of loneliness
I saw what people saw in my work
the blossoming silence I'd grown
to defend myself

Alien Lives

I admire the audacity of the mosquito
Sucking my blood   the impertinence
Of the fly walking across my forehead
Dipping its labellum in my sweat
The monarch stopping for a day
To rest and feed on the milkweed
Before resuming its flight to Mexico
The immortal earthworm pushing
Through darkness   dividing itself
In perpetuity   the moth
Spiraling toward the scorching light

The Bread of Forgetting

The past continues
Waving to me in the dusky light

Every morning on my knees worshipping
Regret / I know what I owe
Is more than I know

The erasures are catching up
To my severed hand
Writing apologies to the dead

Tomorrow merely a theory
Today a broken window

V.

Chrysalis

We think of metamorphoses
As glorious and beautiful
A quiescent
Chrysalis emerging
As a yellow butterfly
Slowly unfolding her
Translucent wings
Letting them dry
In the open air
And flying off
In a flittering arc
Reminding us
Of our emergence from
The chrysalis of self-conscious
Adolescence
Into the less tumultuous
Uncertainties
Of adulthood and of
The final transformation
We yearn for, the moldering body
Releasing the immortal spirit, but imagine
How the wormlike
Caterpillar feels after a life
Of serenely munching leaves
To curl herself
On the underside of a chosen leaf
Secreting a fiber
Spinning a cocoon, incorporating
Twigs, urticating hairs
Fecal pellets, bits of leaf and bark
Disguised from
Predatory bats and nightjars
While the arrival works its magic
And if she's aware
As all things are aware
Rock tree wind

She must feel
Her skin stretching, covering
Her body now
A thing with wings
That doesn't resemble
Hope so much
As grace, the undeserved love
That comes into our lives
As a gift

Dandelion

In the cracks of asphalt,
in the broken ground,
in the abandoned field

of the demolished house,
among the tumble of brick
and block and rebar rising out of rubble,

out of bomb crater and bulldozed gravel,
out of disaster and mayhem,
out of ugly order and disorder,

out of beautiful neglect
wilding occurs, so
on thin white wings

the seed settles
unnoticed,
bringing life to ruined places.

Sun Star

After churning all night
I wake to see the sun star
In the window its perfect
Blossoms full of light
I smell coffee and hear you
Moving room to room
In two weeks we'll transplant
Our sun star to the front bed
Between the extravagant
Dragon flower and the delicate
Hyacinth which Homer says
Sprang from the blood of a boy
Killed by Zephyr god of wind
We'll root the flower well
White threads of mycelia
Will embrace the tendrils
Welcoming and nourishing
As we gradually inhabit
Our lives every morning
Fiercely in love with light

August Song

I can't help but fall in love
With the blissful light of lemonade at noon
And gazpacho in the evening
With a slice of lime hanging by its wound

I trust with all my heart
The hot walk of the girls in flip flops
Headed to the blue eye of the pool

I believe in sweat
The way it hangs from my chin
Falls to the scalding sidewalk
Merges with the breath of men
A cloud rising above the shimmering city
Flies over the mountains and falls in the sea
Rising and falling and rising again

Affinity

Have you ever noticed
When you are pushing
A small child in a stroller
She'll turn to look at
Another child rolling past
And there's a moment of
Recognition, a commonality?

And when we're brushing
A horse, the wide flanks glistening,
The animal will turn to look at us
Its walnut eye half-lidded.
And the dog sitting in front of us
A toy in its mouth
An attitude of expectant excitement,
Inviting us to play? You returning
From Africa and me traveling
At my desk. And later we step
Onto the porch and look up
At the night sky, home at last

Rain

Rain knows more than you think
How it finds the smallest spaces
Between your neck and your collar
How even your eyes are filling
With rain at the memory
Of your brother, your sister, one who refuses
To speak to you, and one who speaks beyond
Her passing by her own hand years ago

Every rain recalls every rain
Sitting at the window as a child
Seeing the trees fill with wind
Pulling at their roots, feeling the rain
Fill the spaces in the soil, quenching
The long memories. Your grandmother
Playing piano in the next room
Improvising riffs in her mania
Absorbed by your body
And now she is calling you
From far away and you know
Her voice how like the rain it is

The Large

Leaves us wordless   breathless
Unable to know what to do
With so much beauty
The blasted oak tree
The golden sky   the view
Of the river from the mountain
All we can say is *Zowie*
But the small urges us
To speak   the rise
Of the sleeper's chest
The breath of night air moving
The curtain   the moon
Hanging its hat on a tree
The curl on the sweaty brow
Of the grocery clerk as she
Counts the cost of our meals

Peony

Bees love lavender
And lavender loves rain

All flowers are miracles
Of course   but the peony
Requires ants to unfold
Its many petals

My story and yours
Are full of terrible choices
And now we have love
In a time of war

And after the rain
The leaves are heavy
With possibilities
We can believe in

The smell of the earth
The stone-like fruit
Of the elderberry
Still green

We had a miraculous
Recovery from
Our obsessions
The grip of ourselves
On ourselves

We were fascinated
By our self-immolation
Tell me, maple tree
Is there a common mystery?

Did you know
On the far side of the moon

The astronauts heard
Weird music?

Becoming staying remembering
Our task is not easy
I hate well-behaved poems
Don't you?

$D = \log N / \log s$

What could be more beautiful than the fractal equations
Of snowflakes, quartz crystals forming infinitely varied patterns,
Cloudbanks on the horizon refracting light, dividing red from blue

In the geometry of the spectrum, the black hole of our deaths
Pulling everything we know into an oblivion that might emerge
In another dimension, the mysterious mathematics of the cosmos

Within us that includes the chemical combinations describing love
But is not actually love, merely one of its many poetries?

Turnip Love

A turnip will never betray you
When you grab it by the green
And pull it from the ground
Its tendrils cling unashamed
To the dirt that nourished it
Shoulders pink from the sun
The turnip reminds me of you
Coming in from the garden
Pulling your shirt over your head

Turnip Greens

You can never be lonely
Washing turnip greens in the sink
The tender ones with the least bite
Picked in May before the root swells
The heavy virtuous stalks   the leaves waiting
Twice for baptism   once in the sink
Once in the pot   Memory
Nourishes like the whole pot of soup
You and your sister ate
Thick with greens potatoes white beans
Soaked overnight out-waiting
Your hunger   You lifted a spoon
To her lips   then yours again and again
Impatient as always she grabbed the spoon
From your hand and the two of you
Stood over the stove laughing eating
Mopping the last of the broth
With brown bread   Then you sat at the table
And talked for hours   She remembered the tall sycamore
She climbed years before   higher than the boys
Happiness far away

Ecstasy

Someone offered me Ecstasy
And I wondered what they had in mind.
Perhaps lying on a beach on the island
Of Antigua, the sun on my skin, a red sail
In the distance soon to arrive?
Cooking a marinara sauce while listening
To Pavarotti reach the high notes?
Waking in bed next to you, light
Slanting across the bed, our love
Awake again after sleeping too long?
Watching you push our daughter
Into the midwife's hands, the tiny face
Squinched against the new day,
An old soul among us again? Sledding
With our son down the long hill
Of his childhood, and years later
Holding him in my arms after
He emerged from darkness
Still alive? My falling on my knees
After the years of worry, thanking
What-is for delivering this miracle?
What is Ecstasy but a blue pill
Of gratitude, a recognition
All I love is an undeserved gift
Slipping away even now?

Envy

I hear an NPR interview
with my friend from grad school
who won a Presidential Medal
and stood on the White House lawn
with other luminaries of our age.
My friend is appropriately
modest about her accomplishment
so I say to my wife *Good for her*
No one deserves fame more
but an ugly little corner of my soul
hates my friend's success
because it makes me feel small
untalented and undeserving. I spend
the rest of the day brooding about
my trifling pathetic life, writing for
a handful of indulgent friends and
former students. After a day of staring
at the white screen of my failure
I hear you come through the door
home at last from the trauma workshop
you teach. You tell me of a young man
who held his dying brother in his arms
after a drive by and how the family
is still grieving years later and how
the workshop has given the young man
a few tools to help his family recover
and then we read an email from a friend
who now lives with her two children
in a refugee shelter in Poland
while her husband is fighting
somewhere near the Russian border
and I think of my own brave brother
in Houston who discovered the provost
of his university has been lying
and stealing and Jack went
on television to speak truth to power

and lost his job. And even my dog Josie
faces each day with the thrill of play
the joy of long walks through the alleys
and faith I'll place a bowl of her favorite foods
on the floor. And then you pull pasta
out of the pantry, I dress a green salad
with care and my self-pity fades
into the evening ritual of loving gestures
and I feel joy and gratitude for the gifts
I've been given in this one small life

Before Leaving

So this is where you are
Now whether you are seen
Or known this is
Who you are now having come
So far without knowing
And now having barely
Been here at all

Only a few small things
You've done and some
You regret but never regret
Opening to love though
You put so much before
Love leaving it for last so
At last you remember

When your children were small
You put aside grasping
To learn to play as now
Opening a door to words
Scattered on the carpet
Now to build a house
To leave behind in joy

Notes

***Ishmael*,** the first son of Abraham, was born of the servant girl Hagar, but Abraham's wife Sarai forced the girl and her child into the desert where an angel came to them with water and food. Ishmael became the patriarch of the twelve tribes of the Arabs.

Persimmon: The fruit tree described here is the *Diospyros texana*, a species indigenous to Texas and northern Mexico which produces a small black fruit similar to a plum. I was raised in a house on the outskirts of Houston with a large garden where I was expected to work every day. I didn't mind because in the house there was always shouting and hitting while outside I could enjoy the peaceful song of cicada and chickadee, the beauty of azalea and flowering pear, the scent of sage and laurel, and the taste of fig, pecan and persimmon. For me, autism was a gift of silence and solitude. I didn't speak until the age of five and then only with a heavy speech impediment, so I developed the habit of observing and listening to the natural world.

The Deed: According to family legend, my Cherokee great-great grandmother whose name I never knew was visited at her son's cotton sharecrop in 1908 by two agents who made her sign over the rights to the land in East Texas which Sam Houston, the first president of Texas, had given to the Cherokee "for all time." Spindletop, the first oil gusher in Texas, had suddenly made the land valuable. She signed over the deed because she was afraid of being taken to the reservation in Oklahoma.

$D = \log N / \log s$ is the formula for computing a fractal dimension, the generative design of reality as we know it.

Acknowledgments

I'm grateful to the editors of the following works for publishing versions of these poems.

Journals:

Alnaked-Aliraqi (online and print magazine published in Istanbul): "Ishmael," "Uvalde;" translated into Arabic by Saleh Razzouk

Kestrel: "Happy At Your Expense"

Live Encounters: "Edge of the Woods," "Halfway Prayer," "Hookah Wink," "Jubal Rising," "My Brother's Hand," "Persimmon," "Second to Last Testament, "Sweet Hatred"

One Art: "Ecstasy," "Envy"

Plant-Human Quarterly: "Dandelion"

Plume: "The World As Sound"

Poetry Box: "Mulberry"

Prime Number: "The Lamp at the End of the World"

Rune: "Sun Star"

Scientific American: "Chrysalis"

Valley Voices: "Bookfair," "Edge of the Woods," "You Taught Me"

Verse Virtual: "Hearth Song for Danusha," "The Skateboarder"

Anthologies:

Jazz and Literature, edited by Mia Funk, published by Routledge (2024): "Forward Avenue Blues (For Katherine Dunham)"

Love Is for All of Us: Poems of Tenderness & Belonging from the LGBTQ+ Community & Friends, edited by James Crews and Brad Peacock, published by Storey Publishing/Hachette Book Group (2025): "Sun Star," "More"

In addition, some of these poems appeared in *Note from the Editor,* my blog published by *Vox Populi Sphere.*

Finally, I want to thank four mentors: Naomi Shihab Nye, Danusha Laméris, James Crews and John Lewis; two editors: Ellen Foos and Arlene Weiner; and two designers: Jean Foos and Dirk Rowntree.

Michael Simms is the author of three full-length collections of poetry previously published by Ragged Sky: *American Ash*, *Nightjar*, and *Strange Meadowlark*. Simms has also published speculative novels; *Bicycles of the Gods* and *The Talon Trilogy*. His poems have appeared in many publications, including *Poetry* (Chicago), *Plume Poetry*, *Scientific American* and *Poem-a-Day* published by The Academy of American Poets. His poetry has been translated into Spanish, Arabic, Russian and Chinese. Simms is the Founding Editor of *Vox Populi*, an online forum for poetry, politics and nature, as well as the Founding Editor Emeritus of Autumn House Press, a nonprofit publisher of literary books. He has been active in progressive politics and community service for many years, currently working as a peer counselor with drug addicts and autistic individuals. In 2011, Simms was awarded a *Certificate of Recognition* from the Pennsylvania State Legislature for his service to the arts. Simms was born and raised in Texas, but since 1987 he's lived with his wife Eva, a philosopher and psychologist, in the historic neighborhood of Mount Washington overlooking the city of Pittsburgh.

www.ingramcontent.com/pod-product-compliance
Lightning Source LLC
Chambersburg PA
CBHW031419160426
43196CB00008B/998